POP WINNERS

PRESENTS

ULTIMATE UNOFFICIAL GUIDE TO

TAYLOR SWIFT

SPECIAL 2025 EDITION

INDEPENDENT 100% UNOFFICIAL

LittleBrother BOOKS

Little Brother Books Ltd, Ground Floor, 23 Southernhay East, Exeter, Devon, EX1 1QL

books@littlebrotherbooks.co.uk | www.littlebrotherbooks.co.uk

The Little Brother Books trademarks, logos, email and website addresses and the Pop Winners logo and imprint are sole and exclusive properties of Little Brother Books Limited.

Published 2024. Printed in the United Kingdom. Little Brother Boots, 77 Camden Street Lower, Dublin D02 XE80.

CONTENTS

Totally TAYLOR

Let's find out all about Pop Winner's favourite singing sensation, the one and only *Taylor Swift!*

FULL NAME: Taylor Alison Swift
DATE OF BIRTH: 13th December, 1989
STAR SIGN: Sagittarius
HOMETOWN: West Reading, Pennsylvania
SIBLINGS: Younger brother called Austin

If Tay-Tay were an emoji, we reckon she'd be this one...

MUSICAL INSPO

As a young girl, Taylor loved country music stars such as LeAnn Rimes and Shania Twain. When she was 13, Taylor's family moved to Nashville, the home of country music. We reckon that was probs the most important move of her career.

FAVE FOOD

Taylor's favourite food is reportedly chicken tenders and her go to drive-thru meal is a cheeseburger with fries and a chocolate shake. Sounds delish!

LOVES Cats

sea urchins **HATES**

DID YOU KNOW?

The story goes that Taylor's parents wanted her to have a gender-neutral name, so they named her after the musician James Taylor. A great choice, in our opinion!

POP WINNERS Thoughts

Here at Pop Winners, we love how Taylor makes her fans feel special. What's your favourite thing about her? Write it here.

BEADED MESSAGE

Taylor's friendship bracelets have broken! Can you find the lettered beads scattered throughout this book then rearrange them to spell the title of one of her songs?

Write your answer on the white beads.

Answers on pages 78-79.

DESIGN BRACELET BEADS!

Design some new beads to add to Taylor's friendship braclets.

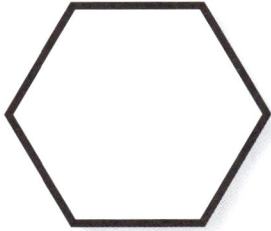

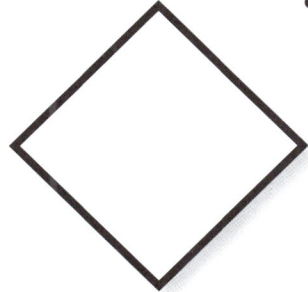

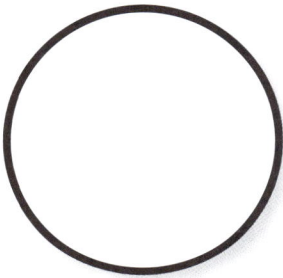

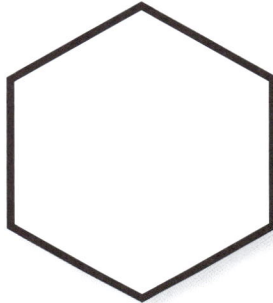

Use Taylor's eras as inspiration for each bead.

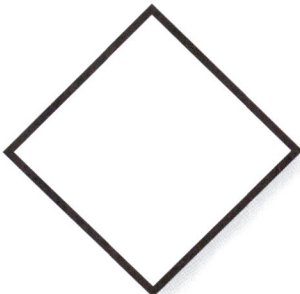

Latest Highlights

Hardworking Taylor never seems to stop. Let's take a look at some of the things she's been up to lately.

RECORD-BREAKING TOUR

At the time of writing, Tay is in the middle of her Eras tour, performing 152 shows across five continents. The first billion-dollar stadium tour in history, Eras includes songs from all of her albums, grouped into themed sets, performed over a three and a half hour all-singing, all-dancing extravaganza. Phew! We reckon this sell-out spectacular will be the pinnacle of her career and can't wait to catch the show!

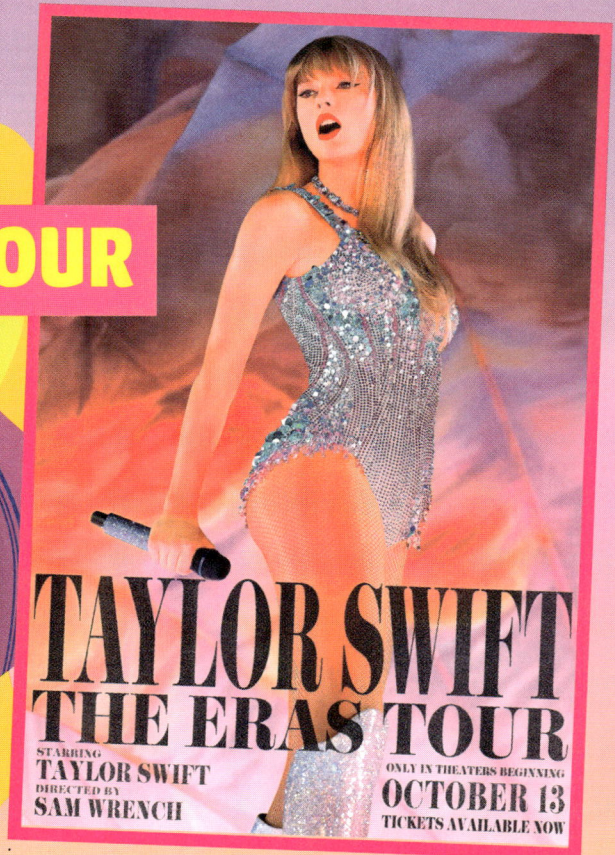

TAYLOR SWIFT THE ERAS TOUR

STARRING TAYLOR SWIFT
DIRECTED BY SAM WRENCH

ONLY IN THEATERS BEGINNING **OCTOBER 13**
TICKETS AVAILABLE NOW

BANKING A BILLION

In April 2024, Taylor officially made it into the Forbes' billionaires list with a fortune reportedly worth $1.1 billion. While she may be rolling in readies, we know Taylor does what she does for the love of music rather than the money and for that, we salute her.

GRABBING THE GRAMMYS!

Taylor made history at the 2024 Grammy Awards by winning Album of the Year for the fourth time. She picked up the award, the top prize of the night dontcha know, for *Midnights*. Tay also scooped the Best Pop Vocal Album award for *Midnights* and was nominated in a further six categories. That aint a bad night's work!

ALBUM #11

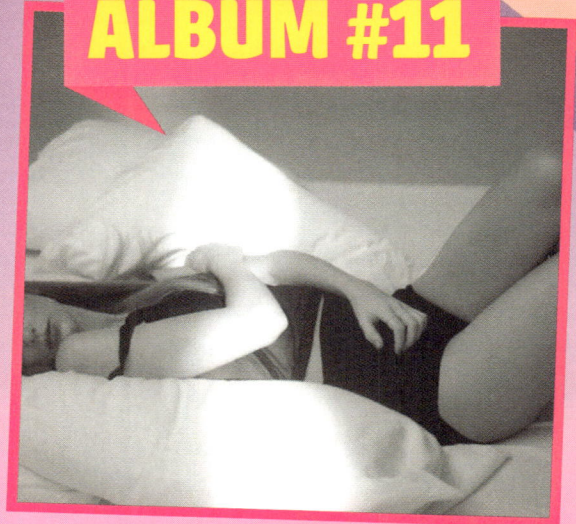

Swifties everywhere rejoiced when Taylor released her eleventh album in April 2024. *The Tortured Poets Department* was an instant record-breaker, becoming Spotify's most-streamed album in a single day. We can't wait to see which awards Taylor picks up for this musical masterpiece.

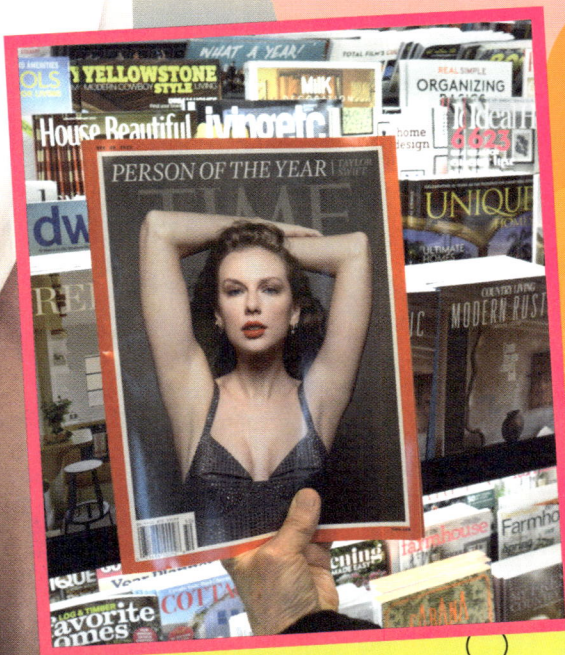

TOP AWARD

Taylor joined former US Presidents, Popes and powerful industry figures to be named *TIME* magazine's Person of the Year 2023. The award goes to the individual who has most shaped the headlines that year, so we reckon the editors made a great choice with Tay!

Album:
TAYLOR SWIFT (2006)

Let's deep dive into the album that began Taylor's rise to stardom, way before being a *Swiftie* was even a thing.

The Beginning

Before her debut album was released, Taylor was just a teen with a big dream. But after years of working hard, writing songs and performing to anyone who would listen, *Taylor Swift* the album introduced Tay to the world. And we were very pleased to meet her!

Promo Trail

Hard-working Taylor promoted her album with a six-month radio tour and by performing as an opening act for several well-known country artists, including her favourite country singer Tim McGraw. How awesome is that?

Rising Sales

Taylor Swift sold 39,000 copies in its first week and as the singer released more and more tracks as singles, sales shot up. In the end, her debut spent 157 weeks in the Billboard 200 chart. We think that's a pretty impressive start, don't you?

Country Influences

Back in 2006, Taylor was all about country music, y'all! The songs in *Taylor Swift* showcased Tay's talent for storytelling and helped make country music accessible to a whole new generation of fans.

Customise Taylor's guitar with a pattern!

T

POP WINNERS Fave

Our fave track on *Taylor Swift* has got to be *Our Song*. We love the high energy and Nashville vibes in this country classic. Can it be our song too?!

TRACKLIST

1. Tim McGraw
2. Picture to Burn
3. Teardrops on My Guitar
4. A Place in the World
5. Cold as You
6. The Outside
7. Tied Together with a Smile
8. Stay Beautiful
9. Should've Said No
10. Mary's Song (Oh My My My)
11. Our Song

Colour the butterflies next to the songs you just can't help singing along to.

11

Popstar Puzzles

How quickly can you solve these Taylor teasers?

WHICH WORD?

Complete these song titles using the words from the list below.

1 Don't .... Me

2 .... on the Beach

3 I .... you would

4 .... Story

LOVE **SNOW**

BLAME **WISH**

POP WINNERS Fave

Our all-time favourite Taylor song title is *Teardrops on My Guitar.* What's yours?

SUPER SEQUENCES

Can you work out which pictures complete these musical sequences?

1 🎵 🎸 🎵 [?] 🎵 🎸 🎵

2 🎤 [?] 🎤 ⭐ ⭐ ⭐

3 🏆 ⭐ 🎸 🏆 [?] 🎸

Images: Alamy

12

TOTALLY TAYLOR

How many words can you make from the letters in Taylor's name?

TAYLOR SWIFT

....

....

....

....

....

....

....

....

....

....

HIDDEN HOBBY

Cross out the letters that appear twice then rearrange the ones that are left to reveal one of Taylor's hobbies.

D E A
G
H F
C
J K
B L M
H
J N
I
M C
D L E
F E

Answers on pages 78-79.

13

TAYLOR LOVES...

From cute animals to musical legends, let's find out about some of Tay's favourite things.

CHRISTMAS

Taylor has always loved Christmas. When she was little, she even lived on a Christmas tree farm. How festive is that?!

PLAYING GUITAR

When she was 10, Taylor was given her first guitar as a Christmas present. The rest, as they say, is history.

HER MUM

Taylor has always been close to her supportive mum, Andrea, and wrote about their relationship in her song *The Best Day*. Awww!

CATS

Taylor adores cats and currently owns three furry friends – Meredith Grey, Olivia Benson and Benjamin Button. We love her choice of names!

14

SHANIA TWAIN

Country/pop singer Shania Twain has been one of Tay's favourite singers since childhood and is a huge inspiration to her.

NASHVILLE

Young Taylor was obsessed with Nashville, where lots of country music legends started out. Imagine how excited she was when she moved there aged 14!

BAKING

Tay likes nothing better than baking up a storm in the kitchen and often shares her recipes on her socials. Chai cookie, anyone?

ICE CREAM

Tay is crazy for ice cream and her favourite flavour is reportedly mint choc chip. That's a Pop Winners fave too!

HORSES

Horses are one of Tay's big animal loves and she's been riding since she was a child.

HISTORIC HOMES

Taylor loves houses with history and owns a period property in Rhode Island called the Harkness House. Let us know if you're looking for a roomy, Tay!

Images: Alamy

POP WINNERS Thoughts

Tay has a great choice in pets – cute cats are our fave too!

Album: Fearless

(2008) T

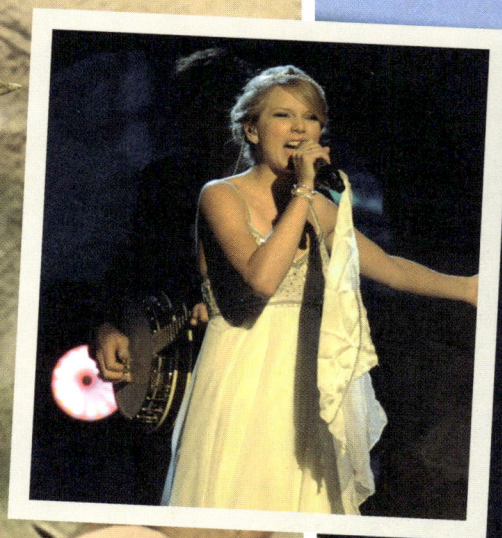

After the success of *Taylor Swift*, fans were eagerly awaiting the release of *Fearless*, Taylor's second album.

Real-life Lyrics

In classic Swift-style, Taylor used her real-life experiences when writing the songs on *Fearless*. Packed full of romance and heartbreak, we love how the stories make you feel like you're taking a peek inside her diary (with her permission, obvs!).

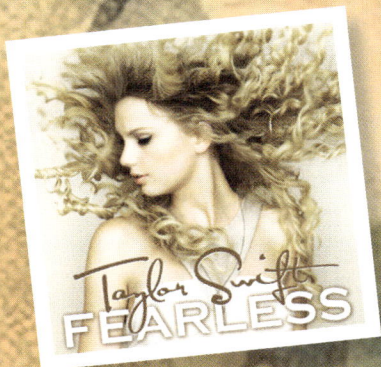

Shakespeare Influences

Reportedly based on Romeo and Juliet, *Love Story* was *Fearless*'s big success. The track reached number 2 in the UK and sold 18 million copies worldwide. Taylor told *TIME* magazine it had only taken her about 20 minutes to write – we think that's pretty amazing!

Gimme a Grammy!

In the first week alone, *Fearless* sold a massive 590,000 copies and went on to sell 12 million copies worldwide. The album also won the singer her first Grammy awards, with Taylor picking up Album of the Year and Best Country Album in 2010. Yaaas!

Taylor's Version

In 2021, Taylor released *Fearless (Taylor's Version)*, a re-recorded album featuring all the original songs plus six new ones. Not only did this new version put musical control back in Taylor's hands, it also became the first re-recorded album in history to debut at number 1 on the Billboard 200. Go Tay!

Which Fearless song do these icons represent?

Answers on pages 78-79.

POP WINNERS Fave

We're choosing *You Belong with Me* as our fave *Fearless* song. It always leaves us with smiles on our faces and we just can't get enough of that catchy tune.

TRACKLIST

1. Fearless
2. Fifteen
3. Love Story
4. Hey Stephen
5. White House
6. You Belong with Me
7. Breathe
8. Tell Me Why
9. You're Not Sorry
10. The Way I Loved You
11. Forever and Always
12. The Best Day
13. Change

Colour the heart next your favourite song.

Images: Alamy

17

Are You a Super Swiftie?

Take this fun quiz to reveal how big a Taylor Swift fan you are!

1 How many Taylor Swift albums do you own?

A Every single one plus all the deluxe and limited editions.

B Most of them.

C One or two.

2 How do you react when a new Taylor Swift album drops?

A Buy it straight away and listen to it on repeat.

B Put some pocket money aside in case I want to buy it later.

C Listen to it at a friend's but don't buy it myself.

3 What would you do if you saw Tay walking down the street?

A Scream, faint and then scream some more.

B Politely ask for a selfie.

C Smile at her as I walk past.

4 Can you name all three of Taylor's cats?

A Of course and I can tell you what they like to eat.

B I know their first names.

C I think one begins with a B...

5 How often do you check Tay's socials?

A Every day. At least twice.

B Once a week.

C Only when she's done something interesting.

6 How many Taylor Swift posters are on your bedroom wall?

A Too many to count.

B At least 10.

C None.

7 Can you sing along to all of Tay's songs?

A I know the words as well as Taylor does.

B I can sing along to the choruses.

C I only know her biggest hits.

8 Do you know where Taylor grew up?

A Yes and I can tell you her zip code too.

B I know the state but not the town.

C Wasn't it somewhere in America?

Mostly As

You eat, breathe and sleep Taylor Swift and know the tiniest details about her life. You are 100% a Super Swiftie! Keep up the good work!

Mostly Bs

You're a fan of Taylor Swift and her music but you're not completely obsessed with everything she does. You're a Chilled Swiftie!

Mostly Cs

You like Taylor Swift and can hum along to some of her hits but you don't need to know absolutely everything about her. You're a Swiftie in the making!

POP WINNERS Thoughts

We reckon Taylor loves all of her Swifties, whether they're superfans or not!

19

Get **creative** with these awesome headwear activities.

Hat Fun!

HAT'S OFF!

On her recent **Eras tours**, Tay chose a lucky audience member each show to join her on stage while she sang *22*. And if that wasn't enough, they even got to wear her hat! While we at Pop Winners love Taylor's plain black fedora, we think it would be fun to zhuzh it up a little. So grab your fave pens and give the *22* hat a **makeover**.

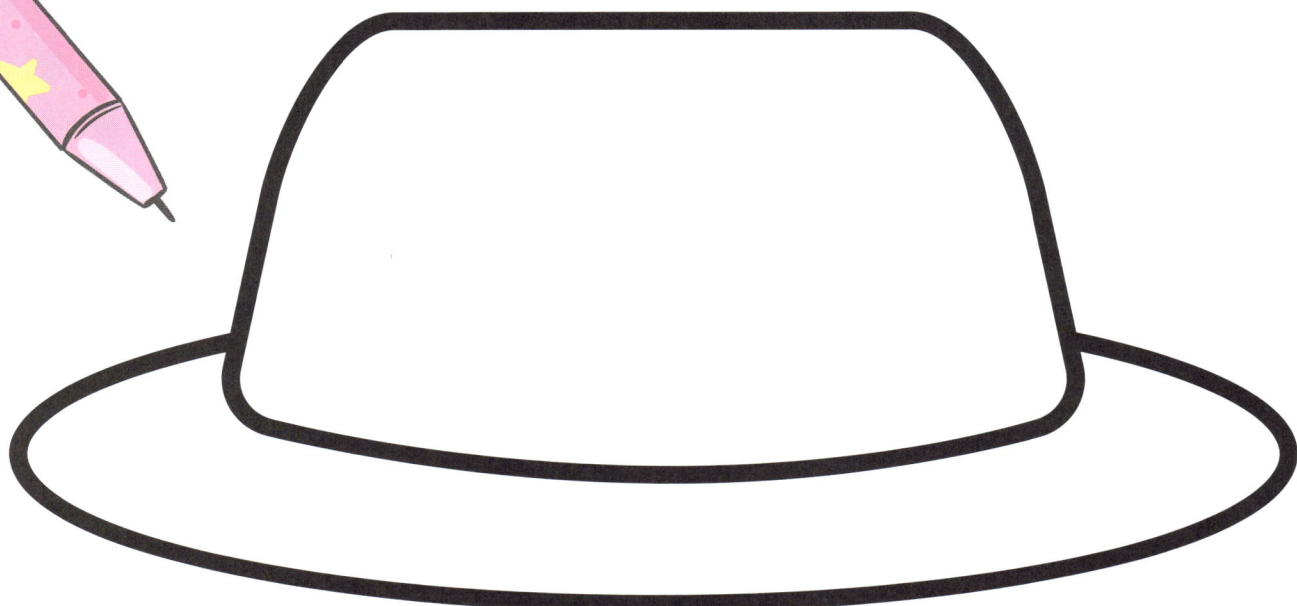

DOES TAY SLAY?

We've trawled through the archives and found these pics of Taylor sporting various hats over the years. But which is your **fave**? Give each one a **rating** out of 10.

/10

We think Taylor pulls off the all-American look to perfection with this cute top hat. Do you agree?

/10

Tay rocks the slouchy beanie in this blast from the past, managing to look both laidback and stylish.

/10

OK, so this graduation mortarboard isn't technically a hat but we think Tay still slays in it!

/10

This feathered military hat from the *Fearless* Tour screams cute to us. Yaaas!

/10

It's not the *22* hat but this little black number comes pretty close. Chic and timeless don't ya think?

OVER TO YOU!

Create a one-of-a-kind hat for Taylor to wear on stage, to a star-studded bash or just to the mall. You decide.

E

POP WINNERS Thoughts

Tay wears hats so well, we reckon she should experiment with other headwear. We'd love to see her rocking a bandana or a 1950s headscarf!

21

Album: Speak Now (2010)

We left teen Taylor behind with the release of album number three but the adult Tay was just as awesome!

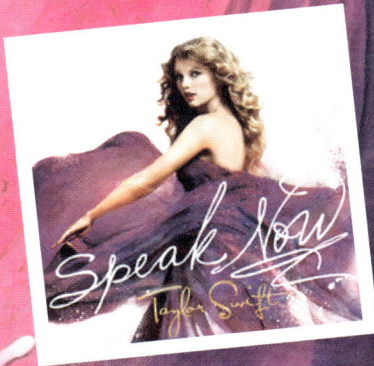

Super Songwriter

Speak Now was a turning point for Taylor as it was the first album where she wrote every song entirely by herself (before that, she'd co-written some of her tracks). We think this album proved beyond a doubt that Tay is a songwriting superstar!

Seven-figure Sales

The album was an instant success, selling over 1 million copies in its first week and spending six weeks at the top of the Billboard 200 chart. Despite now being world famous, we reckon Tay still kept her feet firmly on the ground.

World Tour

Taylor hit the road to promote her new album with the *Speak Now* World Tour. Playing in 17 countries across four continents, fans were wowed with spectacular scenery, eye-catching costumes and, of course, Taylor's high energy performances.

Taylor's Version

In 2023, Taylor released *Speak Now (Taylor's Version)*, which included six 'from the vault' tracks that hadn't featured on the original. Announcing the release on Insta, Tay said the album "tells a tale of growing up, flailing and crashing... and living to speak about it". We. Love. That.

Rearrange the letters that only appear once to spell a *Speak Now* track.

BECMRBNCAR

Answers on pages 78-79.

POP WINNERS Fave

We adore the story of love gone wrong in *Haunted*. And who would have thought violins would work so well in a pop song? Another Taylor classic.

TRACKLIST

1. Mine 🎵
2. Sparks Fly 🎵
3. Back to December 🎵
4. Speak Now 🎵
5. Dear John 🎵
6. Mean 🎵
7. The Story of Us 🎵
8. Never Grow Up 🎵
9. Enchanted 🎵
10. Better than Revenge 🎵
11. Innocent 🎵
12. Haunted 🎵
13. Last Kiss 🎵
14. Long Live 🎵

Colour the musical note next to the song that makes you hit the dance floor.

Images: Alamy

23

EASTER EGGS

It's become a Taylor tradition to hide messages in her songs, videos and even outfits. Here are some of our faves.

Hide it in Caps

Taylor's been sharing hidden capital letter codes in her lyrics and words for years. At first glance, they seem random but when you decipher them, all is revealed! Like when she posted a note to Swifties about *Fearless (Taylor's Version)* and the capital letters spelt out **APRIL NINTH**, the album's release date. Like it!

Say it with Numbers

We all know Tay's lucky number is 13 but did you know she often hides the number in music videos? Like in *Cardigan* where the hands on the clock are pointing to 1 and 3, and in the number 13 graffiti on the wall in *Ready For It?* We'll keep our eyes peeled in future vids for this numerical Easter egg!

Nailed It!

Just before kicking off her Eras tour, Taylor posted a pic of her nails with each one painted a different colour. Swifties were quick to decipher that each nail represented one of her 10 albums (red for *Red*, pink for *Lover*, dark blue for *Midnights*... you know the score). What we want to know is what she'll do now *The Tortured Poets Department* has been released and she's run out of fingers!

Hidden But Not Hidden!

Sometimes Tay's Easter eggs are hidden in plain sight and it's only after an event that we realise she was giving us a clue! Like how the music video for *Me!* featured a huge neon Lover sign four months before *Lover* the album was released. You like to keep us on our toes, don't you, Tay?!

13th Street Station

1989

MISSING
IF FOUND
RETURN TO
TAYLOR SWIFT

KARMA

Get Lost!

We think one of Taylor's cleverest Easter eggs is the 'no scooters' sign in the video for *The Man.* Surely this is Tay's way of sticking it to Scooter Braun who famously bought the rights to her masters from her former record company Big Machine Label Group? Go Taylor!!!

A

Colour Coded Dress

When Tay kept appearing in blue dresses in the final show of the US leg of the Eras tour, Swifties were convinced that she was about to announce the release of *1989 (Taylor's Version)* (cos blue is 1989's colour, of course). And they were right! The announcement was made with an acoustic version of *New Romantic.* Well spotted, Swifties!

Over to You

What are your top three Taylor Easter eggs?

1 ....

2 ....

3 ....

POP WINNERS Thoughts

How many Easter eggs are out there that we haven't spotted yet?

ARENA DASH

Help! Tay-Tay is late for her concert! **Guide** her through the maze to the venue collecting everything she'll need on stage along the way.

START

FINISH

ARENA

Tick off each item as you collect it.

POP WINNERS Fave

The Eras tour tops our Taylor tours list for its feel-good journey through her musical career. Which tour is your number one and why?

Answers on pages 78-79.

Images: Alamy

Era Nail Art

It's time to give Taylor a manicure! Choose your four fave eras and design some awesome nail art for each one. #NailedIt

N

Designed for the .... era.

Designed for the .... era.

Designed for the .... era.

Designed for the .... era.

Album: Red

(2012)

Taylor's fourth album had all the feels and gave her a bunch of hit singles to add to her growing collection.

Feeling Red

Red was the album that saw Taylor move from country star to one of the most famous singers on the planet. Rumour has it that the title came from the emotions of love, frustration and jealousy Tay was feeling at the time. Oooh!

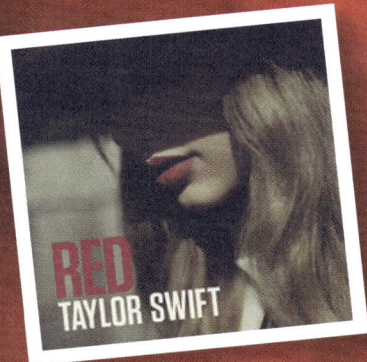

Breakup Album

Years after its release, Taylor told Billboard that Red was her 'breakup album'. And listening to the lyrics in *I Knew You Were Trouble* and *We Are Never Getting Back Together*, we can see what she means!

Big Hits

Out of the seven songs that were released from *Red*, four made it into the top 10 of the US Billboard Hot 100, with *We Are Never Getting Back Together* shooting to number one on the Billboard singles chart. Awesome!

On the Road

The album was promoted with yet another mammoth tour. Lasting over a year, the extravaganza included 15 dancers, a band, multi-level stages, confetti showers and, of course, costume changes aplenty. All of Pop Winners favourite things!

Which one of Taylor's red lipsticks is the odd one out?

a   b   c

Answers on pages 78-79.

POP WINNERS Fave

We Are Never Ever Getting Back Together. It might be an obvious choice but we love the energy in this upbeat song. The emotion, the catchy chorus, the lyrics – this Taylor hit has it all!

TRACKLIST

1. State of Grace ⭐
2. Red ⭐
3. Treacherous ⭐
4. I Knew You Were Trouble ⭐
5. All Too Well ⭐
6. 22 ⭐
7. I Almost Do ⭐
8. We Are Never Ever Getting Back Together ⭐
9. Stay Stay Stay ⭐
10. The Last Time ⭐
11. Holy Ground ⭐
12. Sad Beautiful Tragic ⭐
13. The Lucky One ⭐
14. Everything Has Changed ⭐
15. Starlight ⭐
16. Begin Again ⭐
17. The Moment I Knew ⭐
18. Come Back... Be Here ⭐
19. Girl At Home ⭐

Colour the star next to the song that gives you all the feels.

Images: Alamy

29

GO VIB

Grab your fave pens, channel your inner Taylor and add some **colour** to this mindful message.

Taylor in Numbers

Check out some of the numbers that have defined Taylor's career so far.

5

Taylor always puts her most emotional song on track 5 of an album. She didn't realise she was doing this until fans pointed it out and now it's a tradition!

16

Taylor was just sweet 16 when her debut album *Taylor Swift* was released.

12

Taylor was only 12 when she wrote her first song, *Lucky You*. In 2003 it was released as a promo CD. Cool!

300 million

The Tortured Poets Department was the first album to reach over 300 million Spotify streams in a single day. Mind blown.

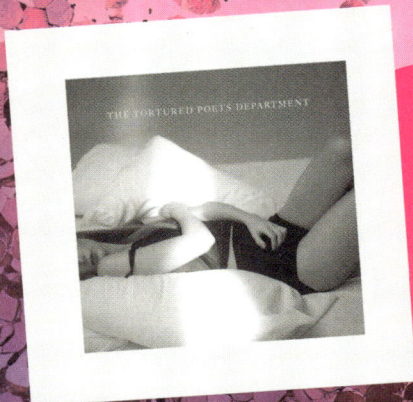

152

The number of shows in Taylor's record-breaking Eras tour. Wish we had tickets for all of them!

11

So far, Tay has churned out 11 awesome albums and we're sure there are plenty more to come.

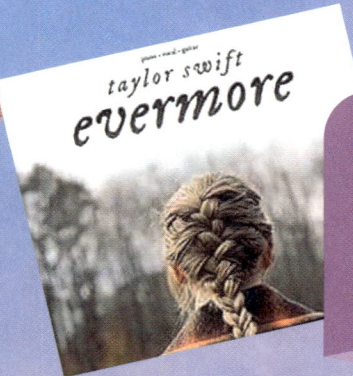

taylor swift
evermore

13

It might be unlucky for some, but 13 is Tay's lucky number, She often writes it on her hand before performances.

345 million

This huge number is the amount of dollars Taylor's *Reputation* tour made. Kerching!

H

10

Young Taylor was just 10 when she was given her first guitar and she's been strumming ever since.

23

The number of VMAs Taylor has won in her career. She only needs eight more to beat Beyoncé who currently holds the most. Come on Tay, you can do it!

Images: Alamy

33

Album:
1989
(2014)

Taylor reinvented herself as a pop superstar with her award-winning fifth album.

Musical Inspo

Named after the year she was born, *1989* saw Taylor dive headfirst into pop music, with her country influences becoming a thing of the past. While we love the Nashville vibes of her earlier songs, we reckon pop is what Tay does best.

T.S.   1989

The Big Apple

Following a marketing campaign in New York, Taylor announced the launch of *1989* from the top of the Empire State Building. We think this was her coolest album drop yet.

Awesome Sales

1989 sold over a million copies in its first week and spent 11 weeks at the top of the Billboard 200 chart. By this point, it seemed that everything Taylor touched turned to gold.

Tour Time

No Taylor album release would be complete without a world tour and the *1989* tour saw Taylor strutting her stuff to over 2.2 million fans in 85 sell-out shows. As well as showcasing her new songs, Tay also included songs from her back catalogue.

Add a pattern to customise these sunglasses for Taylor.

POP WINNERS Fave

Out of the Woods. We love the 80s sound in this emotional song and can't help singing along to the repetitive chorus that sticks in your head for days!

TRACKLIST

1. Welcome to New York 👍
2. Blank Space 👍
3. Style 👍
4. Out of the Woods 👍
5. All You Had to Do Was Stay 👍
6. Shake It Off 👍
7. I Wish You Would 👍
8. Bad Blood 👍
9. Wildest Dreams 👍
10. How You Get the Girl 👍
11. This Love 👍
12. I Know Places 👍
13. Clean 👍

Which song gets a thumbs-up from you?

Images: Alamy

Dressed to Impress

Which of Taylor's looks is your fave? Check out these outfits then circle an emoji to rate each one.

We're loving this look for Tay-Tay – laidback and stylish with just the right amount of cool.

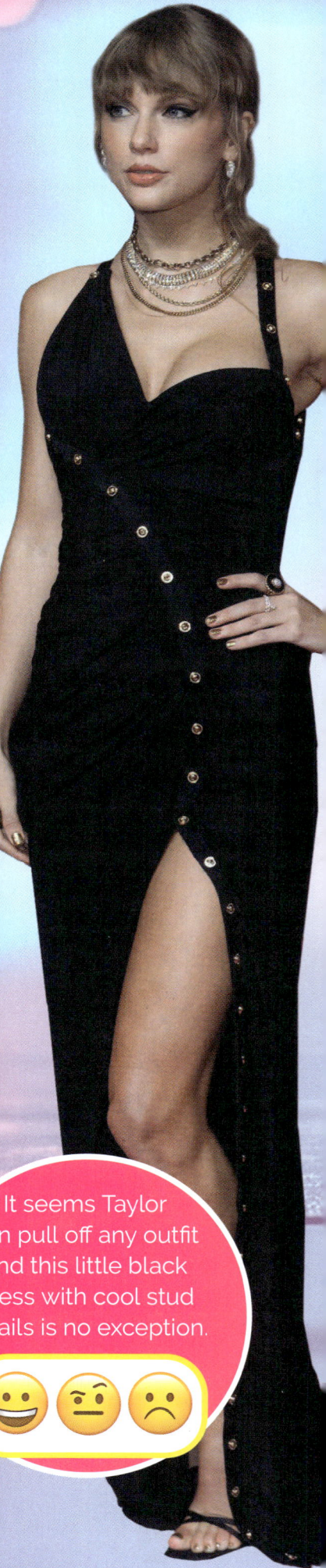

😀 🤨 🙁

Taylor's red carpet ready in this sparkly top and skirt combo. We just want to know what shoes she's wearing under there!

😀 🤨 🙁

It seems Taylor can pull off any outfit and this little black dress with cool stud details is no exception.

😀 🤨 🙁

Is there anything this girl doesn't look good in? Even dressed in bin bags, we think she'd style it out!

V

Tay definitely stands out from the crowd in this shimmering number. Green is a bold choice but she totally owns it.

😀 🤨 ☹️

This is one of our fave outfits from the Eras tour – you wouldn't wear it to the school disco but on stage it rocks!

😀 🤨 ☹️

We love a jumpsuit and this one is the perfect mix of casual and glam. Plus she gets extra points for the matching shoes!

😀 🤨 ☹️

Images: Alamy

#TOTALLY TRENDING

Taylor is queen of the socials! Here's a round-up some of Pop Winner's fave @taylorswift Insta posts.

How excited were we when Taylor dropped this announcement about TTPD being a double album? Super is the answer!

taylorswift ✓ It's a 2am surprise: The Tortured Poets Department is a secret DOUBLE album. ✌️ I'd written so much tortured poetry in the past 2 years and wanted to share it all with you, so here's the second installment of TTPD: The Anthology. 15 extra songs. And now the story isn't mine anymore... it's all yours. 💙

We love spotting the celebs in this star-studded pic taken at Tay's 34th birthday party. Please can we come next year?

taylorswift ✓ Can't believe this year... actually... happened? Thank you for all your beautiful birthday wishes yesterday. 🥺

This empowering post is from the day Tay's first own version album came out. Definitely one to remember.

taylorswift ✓ It was the night things changed. Fearless (Taylor's Version) is out now 💛

PERSON OF THE YEAR | TAYLOR SWIFT

Having a new post pop up from @taylorswift always brightens up our day!

This post about her cats is totally Taylor – so funny and probably actually true!

taylorswift ✔ Time Magazine: We'd like to name you Person of the Yea-

Me: Can I bring my cat.

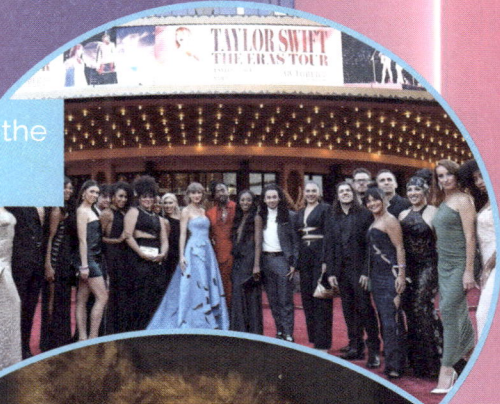

Awww. Look at Taylor and her 'clique' all dressed up for the premiere of *Taylor Swift: The Eras Tour*. Love. It.

taylorswift ✔ the whole clique snapped 🔥

Gotta love a 'fan wearing the 22 hat' post! Taylor Swift gold.

taylorswift ✔ After years of wanting to play in Mexico City, just got to play 4 of the most unforgettable shows for the most beautiful and generous fans. Feeling so grateful for the memories we're making together on this tour 🥹 TE AMO. 🇲🇽

Never one to take herself too seriously, we adore this NYE post of Tay dressed up as what looks like a fierce brown bear! As you do!

taylorswift ✔ bye 2020, it's been weird.
174 w

It would be so much fun to be in Taylor's squad as we think this post celebrating Independence Day proves!

taylorswift ✔ Happy belated Independence Day from your local neighborhood independent girlies 😎

39

Album: Reputation

(2017)

The world waited a long time for Taylor's fifth album but we think it was worth it!

A Long Wait

After the *1989* world tour, Taylor felt the need to take a break so she laid low for a while and focused on writing *Reputation*. The songs on the album were reportedly inspired by her difficult relationship with the media at the time.

New Sound

Never one to churn out the same old stuff, the tracks on *Reputation* had a new sound, which saw Taylor experiment with synthesisers and manipulated vocals. The 'electropop' vibe on this album gets a big thumbs up from Pop Winners!

Record-breaking Sales

Reputation reached number one in the US, the UK, Canada and Australia. By the end of 2017, it had sold a massive 4.5 million copies, becoming the world's best-selling album by a female artist. Go Taylor!

Tour Time

Taylor choose not to do any press interviews to promote the release of *Reputation* but, of course, there was a tour! The 53-show extravaganza was the most elaborate yet with light shows, pyrotechnics and more dancers than ever before.

Which of Taylor's microphones is the odd one out?

a

b

c

Answers on pages 78-79.

POP WINNERS Fave

Dancing with Our Hands Tied.
The catchy dance beat and sentimental lyrics hit the spot for us. We just wish Taylor would come clean and tell us which of her exes it's about!

TRACKLIST

Colour the smiley face next to the song that always gets stuck in your head.

1. Ready For It? ☺
2. End Game ☺
3. I Did Something Bad ☺
4. Don't Blame Me ☺
5. Delicate ☺
6. Look What You Made Me Do ☺
7. So It Goes ☺
8. Gorgeous ☺
9. Getaway Car ☺
10. King of My Heart ☺
11. Dancing with Our Hands Tied ☺
12. Dress ☺
13. This Is Why We Can't Have Nice Things ☺
14. Call It What You Want ☺
15. New Year's Day ☺

Images: Alamy

41

MEET THE SWIFT SQUAD

Taylor has said that she didn't have many friends when growing up but she's more than made up for it now. Let's meet some of her squad...

Sabrina Carpenter

When Sabrina Carpenter sang Taylor Swift songs on YouTube as a child we bet she never dreamed she'd one day be friends with her – but that's exactly what happened! The pair are often spotted out and about together and Sabrina opened for Tay on the first leg of her Eras tour.

Gigi Hadid

Taylor's friendship with model Gigi goes way back and the pair have been papped everywhere, from hanging out in NYC to hiking in LA. And, of course, Gigi has popped up in one of Tay's videos (*Bad Blood*) and been a surprise guest on tour. We love the perks of being in the Swift Squad!

Lana Del Rey

Singer Lana duetted with Tay on Taylor's track *Snow on the Beach*. They were both up for Album of the Year at the 2024 Grammys (which could have been totally awks) but after Taylor was announced as the winner, she dragged Lana on stage with her and everything was fine!

Ice Spice

Rapper Ice Spice is one of the newest members of Taylor's squad. The pair first teamed up in 2023 for a remix of Taylor's song *Karma* and Ice joined Tay as a surprise guest for one of her Eras shows. These two seem as close as sisters and we love that!

Blake Lively

Actor Blake Lively has been in Taylor's squad since 2015. Blake directed the music video for Tay's *I Bet You Think About Me* and Taylor name checked Blake's three kids, James, Inez and Betty, in the song *Betty*. Cute!

Selena Gomez

Taylor met actor and singer Selena Gomez in 2008 when they were both dating a Jonas Brother. The pair have stayed close friends ever since and Selena even made an appearance in Tay's *Bad Blood* video. That's so cool!

Images: Alamy

43

Say it with a Bracelet

Join the scores of Swifties who swapped friendship bracelets at the Eras tour and make your own to trade with a friend.

What's Behind the Bracelets?

"So, make the friendship bracelets, take the moment and taste it," Taylor sang in *You're on Your Own, Kid* and making and swapping friendship bracelets at the Eras tour swiftly became a Swiftie must-do! Usually made of coloured beads spelling out a song title, album title or message, the internet is now awash with tutorials on how to make the perfect wristwear.

You Will Need

- ✓ Thin elastic
- ✓ Scissors
- ✓ Sticky tape
- ✓ Coloured beads
- ✓ Letter beads

Adult guidance is needed for this activity.

How to Make

1. Plan out your design and lay the beads in the right order on a flat surface.

2. Cut a piece of elastic, about 30cm long, and use sticky tape to stick one end to a solid surface, such as a table, to stop your beads spilling off the end.

3. Thread your letter beads onto the elastic first to spell out your word or message.

4. Then add coloured beads either side of the letter beads to complete your bracelet. Don't forget to use sticky tape to stop spills!

5. Carefully unstick your bracelet and check the length around your wrist. Add more beads or take some beads off if necessary.

6. When you're happy with the length, tie the two ends of the elastic together in a double knot. Make sure the knot is tight and the beads sit snuggly.

7. Use scissors to cut off any excess elastic and your handmade friendship bracelet is ready to swap!

Images: Alamy

POP WINNERS Thoughts

We love the nostalgic vibe of these old skool bracelets. Even though it wasn't Tay herself who started the craze, they are totally her!

Message Inspo

Stuck for ideas? Then try one of these!

- ✓ SWIFTIE
- ✓ TAYLOR'S VERSION
- ✓ ERAS TOUR
- ✓ YBWM (you belong with me)
- ✓ IKYWT (I knew you were trouble)
- ✓ LWYMMD (look what you made me do)

45

Album: Lover

(2019)

Taylor's sixth album was the first one she truly owned so its release was a huge turning point in her career.

All Taylor

After 12 years of working with Big Machine, Taylor's contract was up and she signed with Republic records. She would now own the masters to all of her new work, starting with the *Lover* album. Pop Winners salutes Taylor for taking back control!

Chart Topper

Lover gave Taylor her sixth number one album in the US and topped the charts in loads of other countries. The album sold 3.2 million copies in 2019 making Taylor the best-selling musician in the world that year. Woo-hoo!

Grammy Groan

As well as huge worldwide sales, *Lover* gave Taylor a trio of Grammy nominations. We still haven't got over the fact that she didn't win any prizes on the night! Sob.

Cancelled Tour

With her tried and tested formula, Taylor had been due to promote the album with a tour. But she was forced to cancel her plans when Covid-19 put the world into lockdown.

Rearrange the letters to reveal a track from Lover.

GAFTLOWER

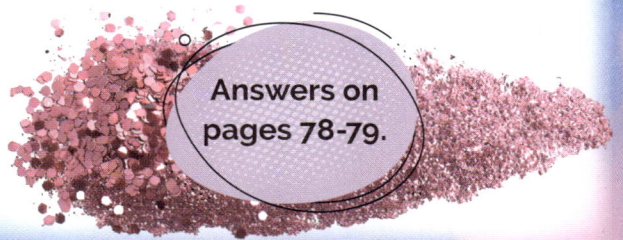

Answers on pages 78-79.

POP WINNERS Fave

The Archer. We love this slow-burning track more and more every time we hear it. The honest lyrics, the whispering vocals, the drum that sounds like a heartbeat – what's not to like?

TRACKLIST

1. I Forgot That You Existed ♡
2. Cruel Summer ♡
3. Lover ♡
4. The Man ♡
5. The Archer ♡
6. I Think He Knows ♡
7. Miss Americana & The Heartbreak Prince ♡
8. Paper Rings ♡
9. Cornelia Street ♡
10. Death by a Thousand Cats ♡
11. London Boy ♡
12. Soon You'll Get Better ♡
13. False God ♡
14. You Need to Calm Down ♡
15. Afterglow ♡
16. Me! ♡
17. It's Nice to Have a Friend ♡
18. Daylight ♡

Colour the heart next your favourite song.

Images: Alamy

Rules for Life

Taylor knows a thing or two about living her best life. Read on for inspo to do the same!

WORK HARD FOR YOUR DREAMS

From when she was a little girl, Taylor knew what she wanted and went for it. She learnt how to play the guitar, wrote songs, made CDs of her music to give to record companies and performed anywhere she could – all before she was even a teenager! She worked hard to make her dreams come true and still works just as hard now she's a superstar. For that, we salute her.

DO THINGS YOUR WAY

Taylor has never been afraid to do things differently and stand out from the crowd. At school, when her classmates were mean to her for loving country music instead of pop, Taylor didn't let that stop her following her dream of becoming a country music singer. We think the resilience she showed at such a young age has got her where she is today. Keep doing things your way, Tay!

Tick the three words you think best describe Taylor.

- ✓ **FIERCE**
- ✓ **THOUGHTFUL**
- ✓ **CONFIDENT**
- ✓ **KIND**
- ✓ **TALENTED**
- ✓ **HARDWORKING**
- ✓ **FUNNY**
- ✓ **CREATIVE**

Write down the three words that best describe you.

1 ....

2 ....

3 ....

APPRECIATE YOUR FAMILY

Taylor has been lucky to have a supportive family in her parents, Andrea and Scott, and her younger brother Austin. She's always appreciated everything they've done for her, especially when the whole family moved across the country to Nashville to kickstart Taylor's singing career. Go Team Swift!

LOOK OUT FOR YOUR FRIENDS

These days, Tay isn't short of BFFs and she's got a tightknit crew of friends around her. They support each other, celebrate each other's successes and are there through the good times and the tough times. We'd love to have Tay as a bestie – she'd be so much fun to hang out with and would always have our back.

How are you feeling right now? Use this space to set your feelings free!

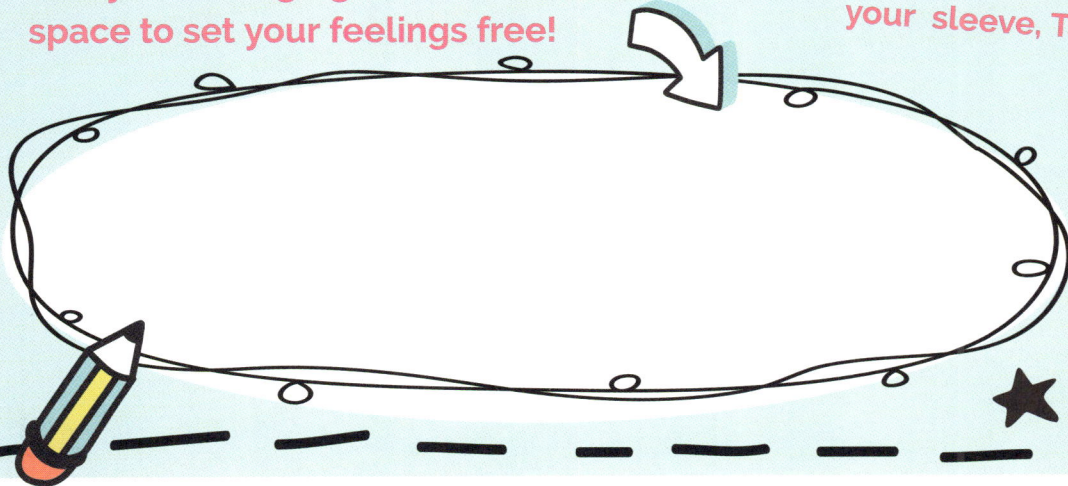

SET YOUR FEELINGS FREE

It's never good to bottle up your emotions so we love how Tay isn't afraid to let others know how she's feeling. As most of her songs are based on her own experiences, her lyrics give us a peek inside her world. Keep wearing your heart on your sleeve, Tay!

Images: Alamy

POP WINNERS Thoughts

Tay seems to be smashing it at life right now. Long may it continue!

Which TAYLOR Are You?

Which version of Tay are you most like? Answer the questions below to find out!

E

1 Which is your fave Taylor Swift song?

- Picture to Burn ✓
- Shake it Off
- State of Grace ✓

2 What's your perf activity?

- Horse riding ✓
- Dancing
- Going to a gig ✓

3 Which instrument would you like to play?

- Acoustic guitar ✓
- Keyboard
- Electric guitar ✓

4 Which outfit would you rather wear?

- Denim skirt and cowboy boots ✓
- Whatever is on trend
- Black jeans and a band T-shirt ✓

POP WINNERS Thoughts

We think we're the perfect mix of all three Taylors!

5

What do you love to hear in a Taylor Swift song?

- Lyrics that tell a story ◯
- A catchy chorus ◯
- An electric guitar solo ◯

6

How would your BFF describe you?

- Kind and thoughtful ◯
- Energetic and smiley ◯
- Confident and loud ◯

Mostly Country Taylor

You're happy-go-lucky and enjoy the simple things in life, like hanging out with your besties. You're country Taylor!

Mostly Pop Taylor

You're full of energy and like nothing more than dancing along to a catchy track or two. You're pop Taylor!

Mostly Rock Taylor

You're super confident, play your music loud and like to stand out from the crowd. You're rock Taylor!

Images: Alamy

51

Album: Folklore

(2020)

Taylor's lockdown album took Swifties everywhere by surprise – in a good way, of course!

Surprise Album

Folklore was written during the Covid-19 pandemic when the world was in lockdown. Taylor worked remotely with writers and producers and managed to keep her eighth album top secret. We didn't know she could be so sneaky!

Insta Announcement

Taylor announced the release of *Folklore* on Instagram writing, "Tonight at midnight I'll be releasing my entire brand new album of songs I've poured all of my whims, dreams, fears, and musings into." Best lockdown treat ever!

Bonus Track

To add to the excitement, Taylor included a bonus track, *The Lakes*, on deluxe editions of the CD and vinyl albums. There were eight editions of each format, with unique covers, photos and artwork.

Grammy Time

Folklore became the best-selling album in the US in 2020 and Taylor broke yet another musical record by winning Album of the Year at the Grammys for the third time. Even a global pandemic couldn't stop this girl!

Design the perfect cardigan for Taylor.

POP WINNERS Fave

Cardigan. The lyrics seem both happy and sad and the song makes us feel like we're wrapped up in a cosy cardi! Yet another musical masterpiece.

TRACKLIST

1. The 1 ✳
2. Cardigan ✳
3. The Last Great American Dynasty ✳
4. Exile ✳
5. My Tears Ricochet ✳
6. Mirrorball ✳
7. Seven ✳
8. August ✳
9. This Is Me Trying ✳
10. Illicit Affairs ✳
11. Invisible String ✳
12. Mad Woman ✳
13. Epiphany ✳
14. Betty ✳
15. Peace ✳
16. Hoax ✳
17. The Lakes (bonus track) ✳

Colour the flower next to the track that makes you think of lockdown.

VIDEO VIBES

Behind every awesome release there's an equally awesome music video. Can you work out which of Taylor's videos these moments are taken from?

1

....

2

....

3

....

4

....

5

....

6

....

POP WINNERS Thoughts

Our award for best video goes to Look What You Made Me Do. We love how Taylor makes fun of herself and the different versions of Taylor bickering at the end is hilare! Music video gold.

Answers on pages 78-79.

Images: Alamy

Super Stylist

FILM PREMIERE

TOUR SHOW

E

POP WINNERS Thoughts

Taylor has experimented with so many different styles over the years and manages to look amazing whatever she wears. Can we borrow her stylist, please?

Taylor's diary is packed full of events. Can you design an outfit for her to wear to each of them?

SHOPPING SPREE

MEAL WITH BFF

Album: Evermore

(2020)

Taylor surprised us yet again with the release of her ninth album, only a few months after Folklore.

taylor swift
evermore

Another Surprise!

The Covid-19 lockdown didn't stop hardworking Taylor and Swifties worldwide couldn't believe their luck when *Evermore* was released just five months after *Folklore*. Two albums in one year, what a treat!

Lucky Number

Evermore dropped just before Taylor's 31st birthday. In a Tweet, Tay told fans that she was excited about turning 31 as it was her favourite number backwards. *Evermore* was her present to the fans who had always supported her.

Tell Me a Story

Described as a sister album to *Folklore*, *Evermore* was praised for its storytelling. We think the low-key vibe of this lockdown album perfectly suited the uncertain times were living in.

Top of the Charts

Evermore sold over a million copies worldwide in its first week of release. The album reached number one in the UK and topped the Billboard 200 charts for four weeks in the US. Not bad at all!

Cross out the words with an odd number of letters to reveal an Evermore song title.

story cowboy ivy like short closure me

Answers on pages 78-79.

POP WINNERS Fave

Willow. Tay triumphs with the storytelling in this sweet song. The vocals and instrumentals are spot on and the track makes us feel lovely and warm inside. Awww!

TRACKLIST

1. Willow ○
2. Champagne Problems ○
3. Gold Rush ○
4. 'Tis the Damn Season ○
5. Tolerate It ○
6. No Body, No Crime ○
7. Happiness ○
8. Dorothea ○
9. Coney Island ○
10. Ivy ○
11. Cowboy Like Me ○
12. Long Story Short ○
13. Marjorie ○
14. Closure ○
15. Evermore ○

Tick the song that gets your approval.

Images: Alamy

59

MORE THAN A POPSTAR...

We all know that Tay is an awesome singer and songwriter, but did you know she has lots of other talents too?

Actor

Taylor is no stranger to the screen. Her first acting role was in the TV drama series *CSI: Crime Scene Investigation* back in 2009 and she's also had roles on the big screen in rom-com *Valentine's Day*, sci-fi thriller *The Giver* and musical-turned-movie *Cats*.

Clothing Designer

To promote the launch of *Lover*, Tay teamed up with fashion designer Stella McCartney to create a new clothing range. The limited edition line included T-shirts, sweatshirts and jackets. If they were still available, we'd snap up every single item faster than you could say, "styled by Swift"!

Director

Not content with simply starring in her music videos, Taylor has directed a whole heap of them too! Our favourites include the surreal *Lavender Days*, Cinderella-inspired *Bejeweled* and *Cardigan*, which sees Taylor playing her piano in a moss-covered fantasy world then clinging onto it in a raging sea, as you do!

Trailblazer

Over recent years, Taylor has earned a reputation for speaking out about artists' rights, social issues and racial injustice. She has also encouraged Americans to vote in elections. We reckon she'd make a pretty good President herself!

Images: Alamy

Voice Actor

Back in 2012, Taylor voiced the character of Audrey in the animation of Dr. Seuss's *The Lorax*. She wanted to be a part of the film as she loved the character. She said at the time, "I've always really been drawn to people with impossible dreams" – we think that daydreamer Audrey defo fits that bill!

Documentary Star

Swifties were super excited to be invited behind the scenes of Taylor's life when she starred in the Netflix documentary *Miss Americana*. Filmed between the time of the *Reputation* tour and the release of *Lover*, we love how openly Tay speaks. Watching the doc is like having a heart-to-heart with your bestie!

POP WINNERS Thoughts

Seriously, is there anything Tay can't do?!

Bake with Taylor!

Adult guidance is needed for this activity.

When Taylor posted a recipe for chai sugar cookies, Swifties whipped themselves into a baking frenzy! Follow these steps to make her famous cookies for yourself. Yum!

You Will Need

- 110g unsalted butter (at room temperature)
- 120ml vegetable oil
- 100g granulated sugar (plus extra for sprinkling)
- 60g icing sugar
- 1 large egg
- 2 teaspoons vanilla extract
- 1 chai teabag
- 250g plain flour
- ½ teaspoon bicarbonate of soda
- ½ teaspoon salt

For the icing:
- 120g icing sugar
- ¼ teaspoon ground nutmeg
- ¼ teaspoon ground cinnamon (plus extra for sprinkling)
- 3 tablespoons whole milk

How to Make: Cookies

1 Preheat the oven to 180°C/160°C fan/gas mark 4 and line a baking tray with baking paper.

2 Mix the butter with the vegetable oil then add the sugar, icing sugar, egg and vanilla extract. Tear open the chai teabag and add the leaves to your mixture.

3 Mix well until everything is combined – you can do this by hand but if you have a mixer it'll make things easier.

4 Add the flour, bicarbonate of soda and salt and mix everything together with a wooden spoon to make a soft dough.

How to Make: Icing

1 Mix the icing sugar, nutmeg, cinnamon and milk together in a bowl to make a spreadable icing.

2 Spread the icing on top of the cookies then sprinkle cinnamon on top of the icing.

3 Leave the icing to harden a bit and your cookies are ready to eat. At last!

POP WINNERS Thoughts

We love Tay's chai sugar cookies and could literally eat them all day long! Adding chai to the original recipe was a stroke of genius and gives the cookies that little extra spice. Delish.

Over to You

What do you think about Tay's cookies?
Colour the stars to rate the cookies out of five.

5 Put the dough in the fridge for an hour or in the freezer for 15 minutes to make it easier to handle.

6 Dollop a tablespoon of dough onto the lined baking tray and press it down with your fingers until it's about 1/2cm thick. Repeat this step with the rest of the dough, leaving about 5cm between each cookies so they have room to spread.

7 Sprinkle sugar on the top of the cookies and bake them in the oven for 8-10 minutes.

8 Once cooked, leave your cookies on the baking tray to cool for at least 10 minutes, then transfer them to a rack to cool completely before icing.

Album: Midnights (2022)

Taylor's tenth album was yet another musical triumph. Go Team Swift!

Midnights

Late Night Journey

Taylor reportedly wrote the songs for *Midnights* in the middle of the night and described the process as, "a journey through terrors and sweet dreams". We love it when Tay's album titles have a story behind them. 😃

Exciting Announcement

Taylor announced the release of *Midnights* at the 2022 MTV Video Music Awards by saying, "I thought it might be a fun moment to tell you that my brand new album comes out on October 21st". Cue huge screams from the audience and Swifties watching at home!

Let Fate Decide

In one of our favourite album promotions ever, Taylor announced the tracklist for *Midnights* in a series of TikTok videos called *Midnights Mayhem With Me*. These fun videos saw Taylor randomly drawing a number from a bingo tombola before revealing the song title.

Winning Big

Midnights swept the board at the 2023 MTV Video Music Awards, with Tay collecting an impressive seven awards for the album, including Album of the Year and Song of the Year for *Anti-Hero*. That's pretty good going!

Give Taylor's phone case a Midnights makeover.

POP WINNERS Fave

You're on Your Own, Kid. We love the honest lyrics, catchy melody and upbeat tempo in this song about growing up. Definitely one to play on repeat!

TRACKLIST

1. Lavender Haze 🌙
2. Maroon 🌙
3. Anti-Hero 🌙
4. Snow on the Beach 🌙
5. You're on Your Own, Kid 🌙
6. Midnight Rain 🌙
7. Question...? 🌙
8. Vigilante Sh*t 🌙
9. Bejeweled 🌙
10. Labyrinth 🌙
11. Karma 🌙
12. Sweet Nothing 🌙
13. Mastermind 🌙

Colour the moon next to the song that you just can't live without.

Dance Party!

Grab your BFFs, turn up the volume and create a unique dance routine for your favourite Taylor Swift song.

You Will Need

- ✓ Taylor Swift songs
- ✓ Scissors
- ✓ A hat or a bowl
- ✓ Your BFFs

Adult guidance is needed for this activity.

If you don't want to cut up your book, copy the dance moves onto a piece of paper instead.

E

POP WINNERS Thoughts

What's the best Taylor Swift song to dance to? In our opinion, it's gotta be **Shake It Off**. Whether you're shaking, strutting or waving your hands in the air, you can totally go for it with this catchy tune.

Instructions

1 Cut out the dance moves on the opposite page, fold the strips of paper and put them in a hat or bowl.

2 Give the strips of paper a good mix then put on your fave Taylor Swift song.

3 One person pulls out a dance move and everyone has to perform that move.

4 Then another person pulls out a dance move – perform this one and repeat the previous move.

5 Keep taking it in turns to pull out a dance move to perform. Repeat the previous moves so your routine gets longer each time.

6 Keep dancing until the song ends then put the strips of paper back in the hat or bowl, choose another Taylor song and start again.

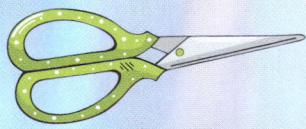

Dance moves

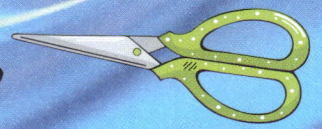

- SHAKE YOUR HEAD
- SWISH YOUR HAIR
- RAISE BOTH HANDS IN THE AIR
- Kick your right leg
- KICK YOUR LEFT LEG
- Nod your head in time to the music
- TWIRL AROUND
- CLAP YOUR HANDS
- Freestyle
- DO THE FLOSS
- SLIDE TO THE RIGHT
- Slide to the left
- JUMP UP AND DOWN
- STRIKE A POSE
- Raise your right hand
- RAISE YOUR LEFT HAND
- MAKE A HEART SHAPE WITH YOUR HANDS
- PUT YOUR HANDS ON YOUR HIPS
- Tip your head backwards
- Take two steps back
- Step to the right
- Step to the left
- WAVE YOUR ARMS IN THE AIR
- FALL TO YOUR KNEES

TAYLOR SAYS....

We've been inspired by Taylor's wise words for years. Here's a Pop Winners round-up of our top Tay quotes.

Colour the heart next to your favourite quote.

"If you're lucky enough to be different, don't ever change."

"You can't have a better tomorrow if you're thinking about yesterday all the time."

"Anytime someone tells me I can't do something, I want to do it more."

"Happiness and confidence are the prettiest things you can wear and I hope you wear them often."

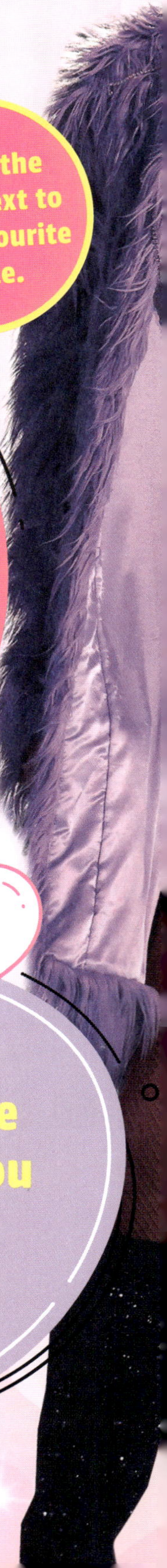

Images: Alamy

68

"In my mind, you should be proud of your mistakes."

"I'm intimidated by the fear of being average."

"People haven't always been there for me but music always has."

"You are not the opinion of someone who doesn't know you."

"Never be afraid to stand up for yourself – sometimes you have to be your own hero."

POP WINNERS

Thoughts

We love how Taylor isn't afraid to speak her mind and call out things that she doesn't agree with. Good on her!

All quotes are taken from *The Big Book of Taylor Swift* by Bianca Burnett.

69

Album:
The Tortured Poets Department
(2024)

In April 2024, Taylor released her eleventh album and this one had the longest title yet!

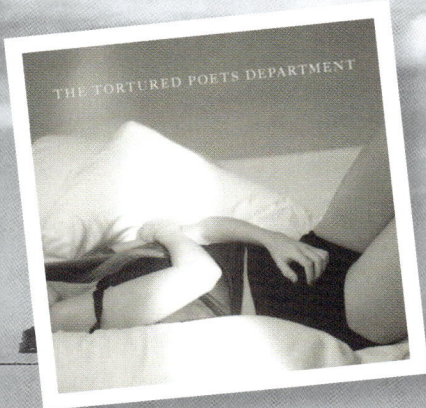

Album Announcement

Taylor announced the release of her latest album at the 2024 Grammy Awards before posting the cover artwork on her socials, along with the caption, "All's fair in love and poetry." It's fair to say, we were hooked from then!

More Songs!

Two hours after the album officially dropped, Taylor surprised us by announcing that *The Tortured Poets Department* was a secret double album and she was releasing an extra 15 songs. Best. Day. Ever.

Cool Collabs

Tay teamed up with other artists for two of the tracks on *The Tortured Poets Department*. Rapper and singer Post Malone added his vocals on *Fortnight*, and indie rock band Florence + the Machine featured on *Florida!!!* We always love a Swift collab!

Record-breaker

The Tortured Poets Department was an instant success, breaking Spotify's record for most-streamed album in a single day and making Taylor the most-streamed artist in a single day. Soon she won't have any records left to break!

TRACKLIST

Colour the star next to the song that you just can't live without.

1. Fortnight ⭐
2. The Tortured Poets Department ⭐
3. My Boy Only Breaks His Favorite Toys ⭐
4. Down Bad ⭐
5. So Long, London ⭐
6. But Daddy I Love Him ⭐
7. Fresh Out The Slammer ⭐
8. Florida!!! ⭐
9. Guilty as Sin? ⭐
10. Who's Afraid of Little Old Me? ⭐
11. I Can Fix Him (No Really I Can) ⭐
12. loml ⭐
13. I Can Do It with a Broken Heart ⭐
14. The Smallest Man Who Ever Lived ⭐
15. The Alchemy ⭐
16. Clara Bow ⭐
17. The Black Dog ⭐
18. Imgonnagetyouback ⭐
19. The Albatross ⭐
20. Chloe or Sam or Sophia or Marcus ⭐
21. How Did It End? ⭐
22. So High School ⭐
23. I Hate It Here ⭐
24. thank you aIMee ⭐
25. I Look in People's Windows ⭐
26. The Prophecy ⭐
27. Cassandra ⭐
28. Peter ⭐
29. The Bolter ⭐
30. Robin ⭐
31. The Manuscript ⭐

Which of Taylor's gold discs is the odd one out?

a — Taylor
b — Taylor
c — Taylor

Answers on pages 78-79.

POP WINNERS Fave

So Long, London. The choir-like vocals at the start make us tingle and the punchy lyrics make us want to shout 'yaaas!'. It's safe to say, this heartbreak song gives us all the feels.

71

QUIZ ME

G

How well do you know Taylor? Answer these true or false questions to find out!

All of the answers can be found in this book.

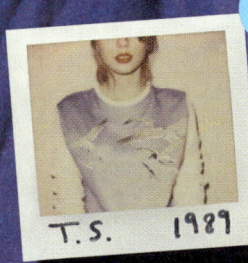

1 *1989* was named after the year Taylor was born.

( ) True ( ) False

2 Taylor has four cats.

( ) True ( ) False

3 Taylor won Album of the Year at the 2024 Grammys.

( ) True ( ) False

T.S. 1989

4 Teenage Taylor moved to Memphis to become a country singer.

( ) True   ( ) False

5 Swifties swap necklaces at Taylor's shows.

( ) True   ( ) False

6 Tay's debut album was called *Swift*.

(✓) True   (✓) False

7 *Folklore* was Taylor's lockdown album.

( ) True   ( ) False

8 Taylor's lucky number is 14.

( ) True   ( ) False

9 Taylor's younger brother is called Austin.

( ) True   ( ) False

10 Taylor described *Red* as her 'break-up album'.

( ) True   ( ) False

POP WINNERS Thoughts

We reckon Swifties have extra big brains to store all their Taylor trivia!

Answers on pages 78-79.

How did you do?

1-3 Sure you're a Swiftie?!

4-7 Pretty good goin'!

8-10 Top of the class!

POP WINNERS

Predictions

We don't know what the future holds for Tay but we've had fun coming up with these predictions! Do you think any of them will actually come true?!

MOON TOUR

Having broken all records with her Eras tour, Tay takes performing to the next level by beaming a hologram of herself onto the moon so the whole world can watch her sing!

MISS AMERICAN FOOTBALL

After months of watching boyf Travis Kelce on the field, Taylor decides his American Football team needs a new strip and designs it herself! Shoulder pads and sparkles go great together, dontcha know!

Images: Alamy

NORMAL LIFE

After reaching the pinnacle of her singing career, Tay decides to give it all up for a normal life. She lands herself a job in a supermarket where she can be heard singing songs about baked beans as she stocks the shelves!

COOK BOOK

Following on from the success of her chai sugar cookies, Taylor publishes her own cook book with all the recipes named after her songs! Shake It Off shortbread, anyone?

BABY SWIFT

Taylor hears the patter of tiny feet when she welcomes a mini Swift into the world. Cue lots of songs about night feeds and changing nappies!

What do you think Taylor will do next? Write your prediction here.

FESTIVAL FUN

Taylor surprises Swifties with an invitation to Swift Fest – a festival for her fans in her own back garden! Now, where did we put our tent?

Design a Tour Bodysuit

Taylor loves sparkles! Create her a new tour bodysuit and matching microphone.

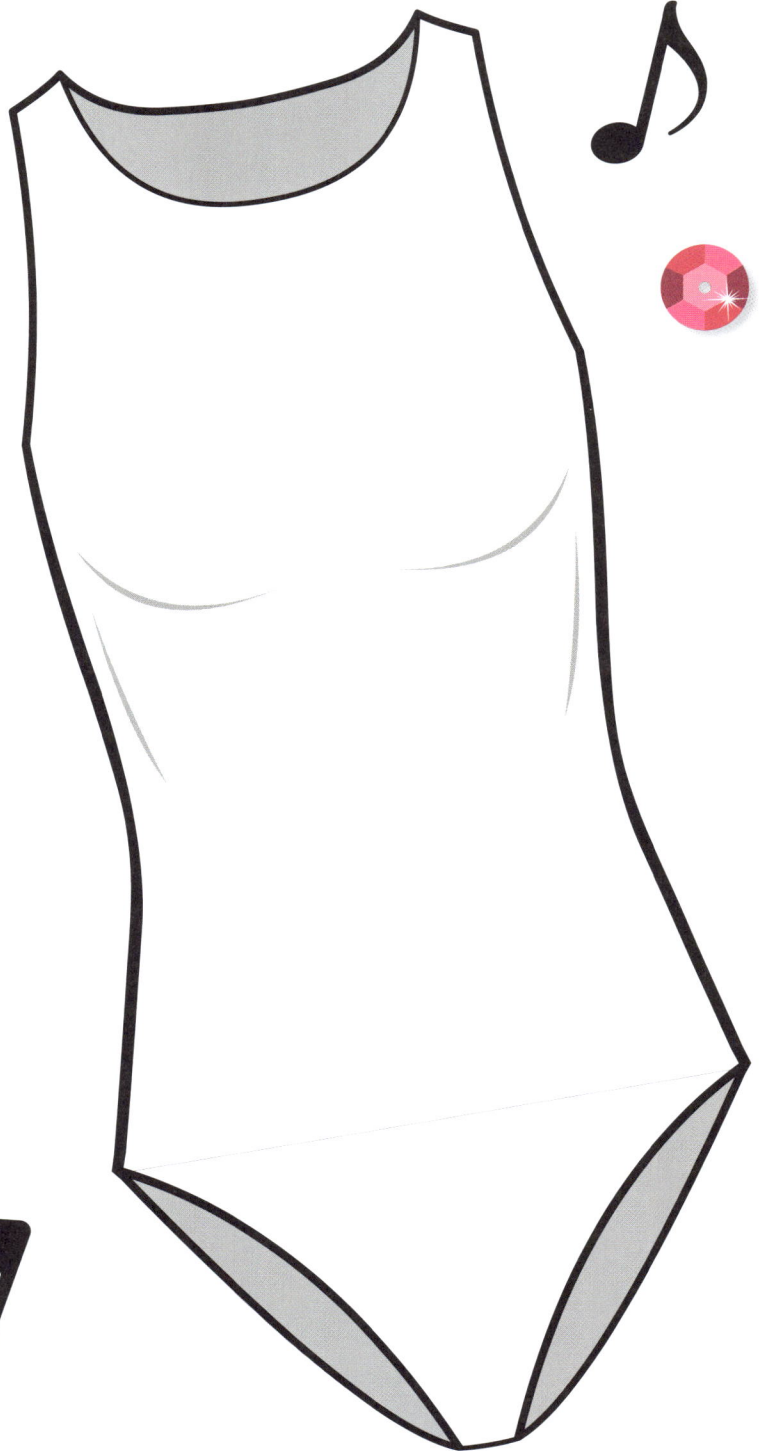

PATTERNS

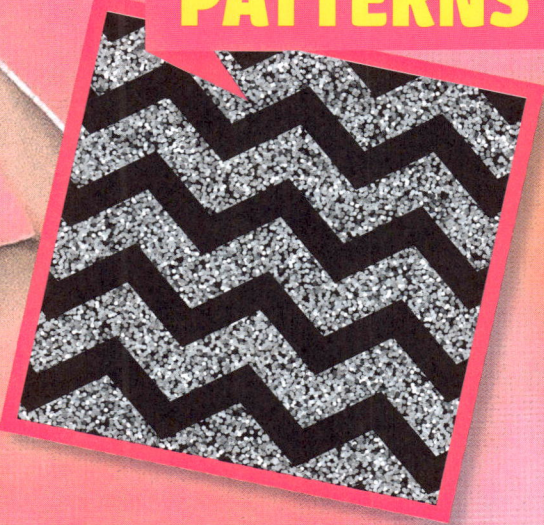

SEQUINS

GLITTER

Use the swatches for inspiration.

Answers

PAGES 6-7

Beaded Message
Better Than Revenge.

PAGES 12-13

Which Word?
1. Blame.
2. Snow.
3. Wish.
4. Love.

Super Sequences

1.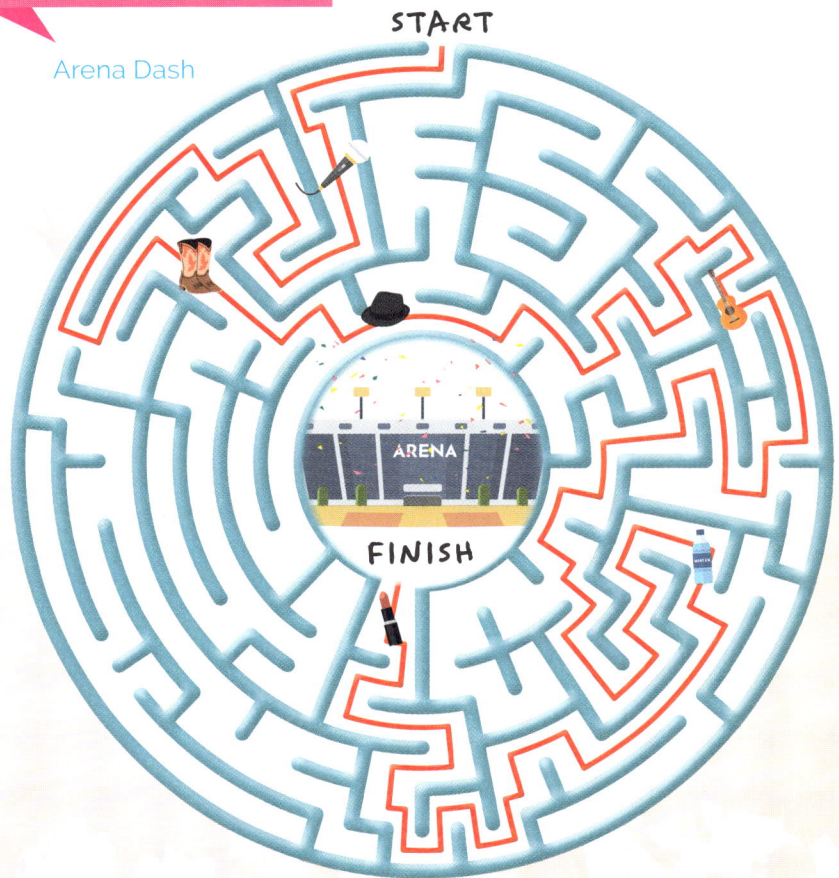
2.
3.

Totally Taylor
Some of the words you can make from the letters in Taylor's name are: lift, rays, sailor, wait, twist and sofa.

Hidden Hobby
Baking.

PAGES 16-17

Album: Fearless (2008)
Love Story.

PAGES 22-23

Album: Speak Now (2010)
Mean.

PAGE 26

Arena Dash

PAGES 28-29

Album:
Red (2012)

PAGES 40-41

Album: Reputation (2017)

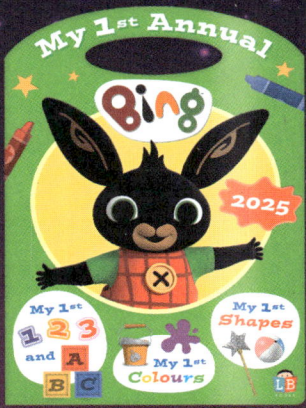

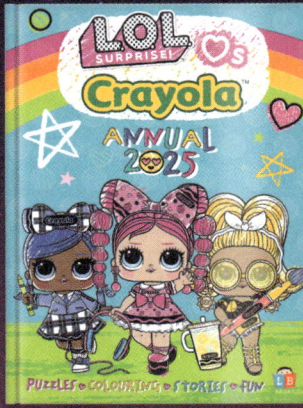

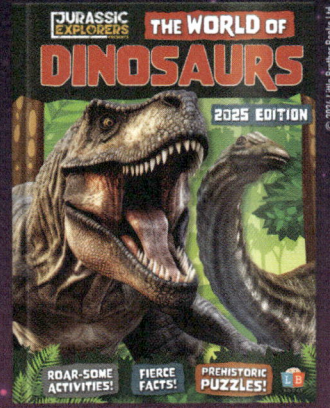

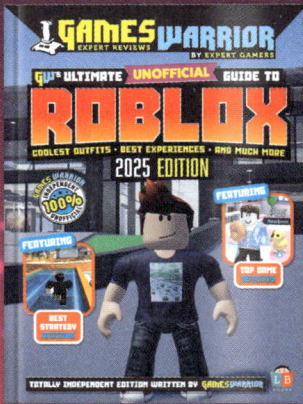

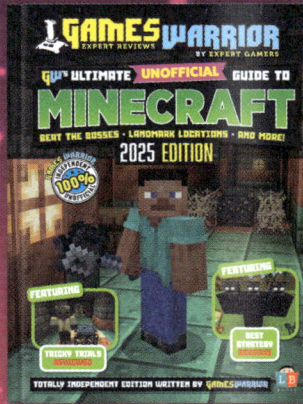

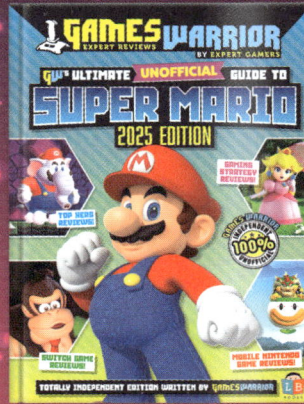

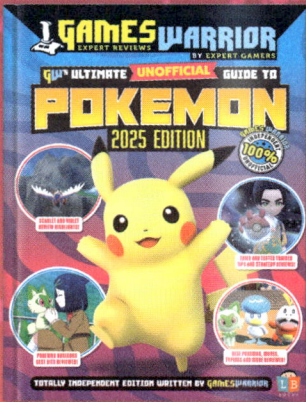

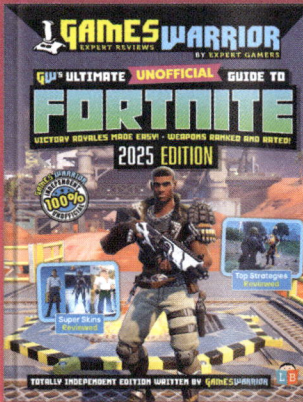

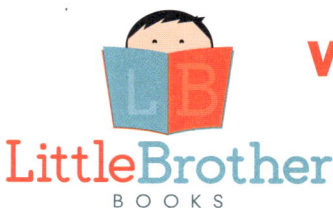